Exploring the 1 WORLD OF

Eagles

Tracy C. Read

FIREFLY BOOKS

A FIREFLY BOOK

Published by Firefly Books Ltd. 2010

First Printing

Publisher Cataloging-in-Publication Data
(U.S.)
Read, Tracy C.
    Eagles / Tracy C. Read.
[24] p. : col. photos. ; cm.
Exploring the world of.
Includes index.
Summary: Fascinating facts
  and full-color photos
ISBN-13: 978-1-55407-647-5 (bound)
ISBN-10: 1-55407-647-1 (bound)
ISBN-13: 978-1-55407-656-7 (pbk.)
ISBN-10: 1-55407-656-0 (pbk.)
1. Eagles - Juvenile literature.
I. Exploring the world of. II. Title.
598.916 dc22   QL696.F32R43 2010

Library and Archives Canada
    Cataloguing in Publication
Read, Tracy C.
    Exploring the world of eagles /
  Tracy C. Read.
Includes index.
ISBN-13: 978-1-55407-647-5 (bound)
ISBN-10: 1-55407-647-1 (bound)
ISBN-13: 978-1-55407-656-7 (pbk.)
ISBN-10: 1-55407-656-0 (pbk.)
1. Eagles--Juvenile literature. I. Title
QL696.F32R42 2010
j598.9'42   C2010-900712-3

Published in the United States by
Firefly Books (U.S.) Inc.
P.O. Box 1338, Ellicott Station
Buffalo, New York 14205

Published in Canada by
Firefly Books Ltd.
66 Leek Crescent
Richmond Hill, Ontario L4B 1H1

The Publisher gratefully acknowledges the financial support for our publishing program by the Government of Canada through the Canada Book Fund as administered by the Department of Canadian Heritage.

Cover and interior design by
Janice McLean, Bookmakers Press Inc.
jmclean14@cogeco.ca

Manufactured by Printplus Limited in Shen Zhen, Guang Dong, P.R.China in April, 2010, Job #S100400150

CONTENTS

PROFILING
Its hooked beak, menacing eyes and broad wings signal the eagle's role in the world: This is a bird of prey.

MEET THE EAGLES

Of the roughly 60 species of eagles in the world, only two are found in North America. Both are members of the Accipitridae family. One is the bald eagle (*Haliaeetus leucocephalus*), which makes its home near large bodies of water and hunts for fish. The other, the golden eagle (*Aquila chrysaetos*), prefers rugged mountainous country, open desert and grasslands and typically preys on small to midsized mammals such as rabbits and prairie dogs.

Despite their different habitat and food choices, though, these two birds of prey have a lot in common. Their size alone sets them apart from most other birds. Each stands roughly three feet (0.9 m) tall and has a wingspan of up to eight feet (2.4 m). Their homes are likewise enormous — massive constructions of branches and sticks that dwarf the tidy grass nests of robins and sparrows.

From a human point of view, perhaps their most impressive shared trait is their flying style. These birds can *soar*. With their wide, broad wings, they float far above us, almost disappearing against a brilliant blue sky, until suddenly, they drop to earth, talons outstretched to snatch their prey.

Humans have come close to destroying eagle populations several times. Still, these masters of the sky endure, a living symbol of high-flying freedom and aerial grace that we earthbound humans can only dream about.

MORTAL COMBAT
A life-and-death aerial competition between these fearless bald eagles will end with a high-speed plunge to earth and a last-minute release of their locked talons.

ANATOMY LESSON

Not all birds are created equal. By virtue of their size, the bald and golden eagles command respect and inspire fear in the natural world. But how do these big flying birds get off the ground?

Despite its oversized dimensions, the eagle shares a basic design with 8,500 other bird species. Its streamlined shape limits wind resistance. Hollow bones, a delicate skeleton and a minimum of body tissue keep it light, yet its framework is soundly built to support powerful flight muscles and withstand the stresses of flying.

As with all birds, the eagle's body and wings are covered with overlapping water-repellent feathers that trap air and act as insulation. The adult golden eagle's are dark brown, with gold at the back of its head and neck. A "booted" eagle, the golden eagle has feathers growing down to its toes. The mature bald eagle's head and tail feathers are white, and its body is brown. Each takes about five years to grow into its adult plumage.

Strong muscles anchor the eagle's sturdy legs, feet and razor-sharp talons. Its hooked beak has a bony core sheathed in keratin, the same kind of tissue that forms our fingernails. Its nostrils are located on a patch of yellow skin above the beak called the cere.

With a cold, steely glare from its large deep-set eyes, this mighty raptor sends a message of uncontested authority over its world.

FIT FOR FLIGHT
Typically, birds replace worn-out feathers each year by molting. But because of their size, the bald and golden eagles can take two to three years to replace every feather.

Built for high flight, the eagle soars on sun-warmed air currents called thermals. But on land, bald and golden eagles are less than graceful: They walk with an awkward gait, and running is usually accompanied by flapping wings.

Body length
The bald eagle stands 28 to 40 inches (71-102 cm) tall. The golden is up to 36 inches (92 cm) tall.

Wingspan
7 to 8 feet (2.1-2.4 m)

Beak
The keratin beak is yellow-orange on the bald eagle, dark gray or black on the golden.

Feather tune-up
Feathers are protein filaments woven along a shaft of keratin. The eagle keeps them healthy and smooth by preening. Using its beak and claws, it spreads oil over the feathers from a gland at the base of its tail.

Eyes
The bald eagle's large eyes are pale yellow, while the golden's are brownish gold.

Don't sweat it
The eagle does not sweat. To stay cool, it perches in the shade, pants and holds its wings away from its body to shed excess heat.

Feet and talons
Three front toes and one hind toe are equipped with sharp curved claws.

Average weight
Male bald eagle, 9.3 pounds (4.2 kg); male golden, 7.6 pounds (3.4 kg). Females are typically 25 percent larger.

Average lifespan in the wild
Up to 20 years

Cruising speed
The bald eagle glides at an average speed of 40 miles per hour (64 km/h), the golden eagle at 30 miles per hour (48 km/h).

NATURAL TALENTS

When you're searching for food from a great height, as eagles do, superior vision is what it takes to get the job done.

Look at the eagle's head. Once you've noted that fiercesome beak, the eyes are hard to ignore. They are very large in relation to the bird's head (they're almost as big as human eyes), and they appear to be in deadly focus. In fact, the eagle's eyes have two centers of focus rather than one, enabling this bird to look both forward and to the side at the same time.

Its eyes contain five times as many light-sensitive cells as do human eyes. As a result, the eagle's vision is several times sharper than that of a person with perfect eyesight. (Even while soaring hundreds of feet overhead, a bald eagle is able to spot a fish darting underwater.) Like humans and other birds, the eagle sees a full range of colors, which gives it an advantage when searching out prey that may be well camouflaged.

As protection for one of the eagle's most valuable assets, a ring of bone encircles each eye to guard against injury. A heavy bony brow acts as a visor, reducing glare and reflection from the sun and water.

All birds have an inner eyelid, known as a nictitating membrane. Every few seconds, this membrane slides from side to side across the eye, cleaning away dust and dirt that might interfere with its vision. (Because the membrane is

EAGLE EYE

Like other raptors, this free-wheeling golden eagle has binocular vision. The ability to focus both eyes at once allows the eagle to judge the distance between it and its quick-moving prey.

TWIN THREATS

Armed with eyes that have two centers of focus, the eagle can see both forward and sideways simultaneously. It can also rotate its head up to 270 degrees, a clear hunting advantage.

transparent, the eagle can see through it when it is closed.) To avoid injury from a jabbing eaglet beak when feeding its young, an eagle parent closes this eyelid.

The eagle locates its food almost exclusively by sight rather than scent. Nor does the eagle possess an evolved sense of taste. This is illustrated by the eagle's style of eating. All raptors eat fairly rapidly once they've seized their prey. Chunks of food move from the mouth to the esophagus and then to a storage area called the crop. There it stays until the eagle returns to its perch to digest its food in peace. A willingness to eat dead animal flesh also suggests that taste is not high on its list of priorities.

It's also unlikely that the eagle detects its prey through sound. It does not hear a wide range of frequencies and cannot pinpoint sound as well as humans do.

Key to its success on the hunt, however, is the eagle's dexterous control of its feet. Swooping down to snatch dinner from the uneven prairie or plucking it from choppy waters is a touch-sensitive skill that demands strength and precision.

SIGHT
The eagle's vision is among the sharpest of any animal.

TOUCH
On the hunt, the eagle's feet and beak serve as hypersensitive touching tools.

HEARING
The eagle's hearing does not contribute to its hunting success.

SMELL
The eagle has a poorly developed sense of smell.

TASTE
No supertaster, the eagle usually draws the line at eating something truly foul.

HUNTING FOR SUCCESS

The bald eagle's taste for fish easily explains its choice of habitat. For the most part, this raptor makes its home along the coast and near the many rivers and lakes of Alaska, western and northern Canada and the southeastern United States. The northern-dwelling bald eagle heads south when freezing temperatures limit its access to food. En route, bald eagles famously congregate to feed on spawning salmon in Alaska and British Columbia. Those with nests in sunnier climates stay put.

The golden eagle, with some exceptions, is largely a resident of western North America, from Alaska through central Mexico. There, it earns much of its living hunting small to midsized mammals in foothills and canyonlands and on open plains, grasslands and desert. It, too, leaves its northern neighborhood when temperatures drop and food supplies fall off. In shorter, local migrations, the golden eagle moves down the mountain in winter to escape the cold at higher elevations.

The warm-blooded eagle needs regular refueling, though it does not have to eat every day. Still, like all hunters, it is constantly on the lookout for a meal. To increase its success, it exploits both its superb eyesight and its flying skills.

While the bald eagle's first menu choice is fish, this raptor has a reputation as a scavenger

GONE FISHIN'

This bald eagle makes a take-out dinner look easy. After spotting a fish from above, the raptor glides downward, then skims across the water, cleanly grabbing the fish with its feet — all without getting wet.

CLAW DADDY

The eagle's feet are covered in scales of keratin. Its three front toes and single hind toe are armed with long, curved claws called talons. While the talons are dangerous weapons, their primary function is to gather food.

and a pirate. It is not shy about stealing meals or gobbling up someone else's leftovers. In fact, the bald eagle routinely engages in midair battles over fish with ospreys and gulls. The golden eagle is also ready to fight other predators for dinner, while birds such as the magpie and raven may bravely return the favor.

On sunny days, low-altitude soaring enables the eagle to survey its large territory on the wing, looking for fresh food as well as carrion (dead flesh). When it spies an opportunity, it dives at high speed with a take-no-prisoners attitude. Even so, the eagle's failed attacks on live prey far outnumber its successes.

Weather, terrain and type of prey all influence the hunting style of the golden eagle. It might snatch up a solitary rabbit with a glide attack, a slow-flying goose with a vertical drop or a squirrel by following the ground's contour, then unleashing a surprise ambush. With a larger mammal, such as a deer, the eagle lands on its back, digging in with its talons and hanging on until the animal drops.

Both the bald and golden eagles sometimes cooperate with other eagles to hunt, but most of their solitary hunting schedule is organized around a perch. Multitasking, they preen and look for food from on high, preserving their energy and swooping down when a likely opportunity presents itself.

WHAT'S ON THE BALD EAGLE'S MENU?

Fish, please. But if that's not available, the bald eagle is willing to eat pretty much anything that moves — or once moved. That includes crustaceans, frogs, waterfowl, reptiles, muskrats and hares. This bird is not a picky eater.

ALL MINE

A juvenile golden eagle spreads its wings over a carcass to hide it from competing scavengers. When capturing live prey, the eagle defends its head by using its talons rather than its beak to deliver the death blow.

WHAT'S ON THE GOLDEN EAGLE'S MENU?

Hares, rabbits, prairie dogs, ground squirrels and marmots make up 80 to 90 percent of the golden eagle's meal plan. It also hunts birds, reptiles and fish. Occasionally, it takes down larger mammals such as foxes and deer.

PLAYING HOUSE

B ig birds need big nests, but as with all real estate decisions, location is key. The bald and golden eagles prefer a site with a view and room to grow, ideally away from human activity. A tall tree or a cliff near water, with good visibility and opportunities for perching and fishing, is at the top of the bald eagle's list. The golden eagle also likes heights and commonly nests on a clifftop or ledge, though a tall tree on its own or at the edge of a forest is also an option. Other considerations can include the nest's exposure to sun, wind and rain.

To impress possible breeding partners and discourage competitors, the eagle takes full advantage of the gift of flight, performing acrobatic aerial displays and vocalizations. Eagle pairs may stay together for several years, perhaps even for life, and they plan accordingly. One to three months before a clutch of eggs is laid, the male and female begin gathering large branches and vegetation to build a nest they may return to year after year. Home improvements are ongoing, which helps explain the nest's impressive size. Some bald eagle nests have been used for up to 35 years, eventually growing to eye-popping diameters of 8 to 10 feet (2.4-3 m)

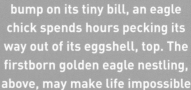

GET CRACKING
Using its egg tooth, a small bump on its tiny bill, an eagle chick spends hours pecking its way out of its eggshell, top. The firstborn golden eagle nestling, above, may make life impossible for its younger sibling by taking almost every meal for itself.

CLIFFSIDE RETREAT

A golden eagle returns to the family nest and its always hungry three-week-old nestling.

HOUSE-PROUD
A bald eagle family
at home in its mammoth nest.
In a few years, this juvenile
will start to grow its trademark
white head and tail feathers.
Until then, it is often
mistaken for a
golden eagle.

and weighing more than a ton.

As home insurance against nest failure, the golden eagle may build a number of nests on its breeding ground. Both the bald and golden eagles often decorate their nests with fresh greenery, which, as it wilts, releases chemicals that kill lice and fleas and act as a natural antibacterial.

Over the course of a few days, the female eagle lays one to three eggs that must be kept warm 24 hours a day. Both parents have a brood patch on their bellies, a featherless area with a network of blood vessels that delivers direct heat to the eggs. Still, the female clocks the most time on the nest, with her male partner delivering food and giving her occasional breaks.

The bald eagle incubates its eggs for 35 days; the golden eagle, from 41 to 45 days. While moving about the nest, the parents may clench their feet to avoid puncturing the eggs with their talons.

In a typical eagle family, two chicks peck their way out of their shells and into the world a day or two apart. Weak, helpless and covered with damp, light gray down, the chicks require warmth and care from their mother. Weight gain is rapid, however, and over the next several weeks, flight and body feathers gradually replace the down. Meal size also increases, with the mother tearing up meaty treats for her offspring. At this time, sibling rivalry for food may turn deadly, with only one nestling surviving the contest.

Within one to two months, a nestling may weigh as much as an adult, though mature plumage is at least five years off. At 8 to 14 weeks, the eaglet is flapping its wings and taking test flights across the nest or to a nearby branch, gaining muscle and confidence. Eventually, the nestling fledges, exiting the nest on its own.

But there is still lots to learn on the risky journey to eagle adulthood. Juveniles may stick close to home for months, honing their flying and hunting skills before leaving to live independently.

THE FIGHT FOR FLIGHT

Trapped for their feathers by Native Americans, shot, captured and poisoned by generations of New World settlers, North American eagles have received harsh treatment at the hands of humans. Even now, we are the major cause of their deaths.

To survive, all birds need habitat that offers secure nesting and feeding opportunities. But human settlements have forced the bald eagle from its preferred neighborhoods along the shores of rivers, lakes and oceans, and we've logged the old-growth forests that once served as its perching and nesting sites. Our efforts to kill mosquitoes using the deadly pesticide DDT in the mid-20th century nearly wiped out the bald eagle species. While DDT was banned in 1972, heavy metals, lead and other pesticides in the environment continue to contaminate the eagle's prey and, in turn, the eagle.

In western North America, wildfires have destroyed much of the shrubland where the golden eagle's four-footed prey once thrived, while mining and energy projects and urban sprawl have radically reduced its nesting and foraging habitat.

Thanks to wildlife-protection laws in both Canada and the United States, bald and golden eagle populations are recovering. But ongoing conservation efforts that protect the eagle *and* its ecosystems are essential to the future of these majestic raptors.

EASY PICKINGS
During the fall salmon-spawning season on the West Coast, juvenile and adult bald eagles gather in great numbers to feed on the nutrition-rich bodies of dying and dead fish.